SCHOLASTIC

MW00353928

TRACING AND WRITING THE ABC's

New York • Toronto • London • Auckland • Sydney
Mexico City • New Delhi • Hong Kong • Buenos Aires

Teaching Resources

Cover design by Jay Namerow
Interior illustrations by Carol Tiernon
Interior design by Quack & Company

ISBN 0-439-81965-2

8 9 10 08 13 12

Table of Contents

Petting-Zoo Pairs (Left-to-right lines) 5

Pretty Ponies (Right-to-left lines) 6

A Rainy Day (Downward lines) 7

Big Balloons (Upward lines) 8

Out Comes the Sun (Slanted lines) 9

Colorful Kites (Slanted lines) 10

Blowing Bubbles (Backward circles) 11

Clowning Around (Forward circles) 12

Wonderful Watermelons (Backward arcs) 13

Fun at the Fair (Review) 14

Lots of Licks (l, i) 15

Ticket Time (t, l, i) 16

Ooh! Aah! (o, a) 17

Dancing Dogs (d, o, a) 18

Crack! Splat! (c, e) 19

Fancy Fireworks (f, c, e) 20

Radiant Rainbow (u, r) 21

Time for a Nap (n, u, r) 22

Bouncing Balls (b, h) 23

Perfect Pumpkins (p, b, h) 24

Jumping Goats (g, j) 25

A Quarter a Quack (q, g, j) 26

Music Makers (m, s) 27

A Vulture's Yo-Yo (v, y) 28

What Time Is It? (w, v, y) 29

Box Kites (k, x) 30

Zooming Along (z, k, x) 31

Ice-Cold Lemonade (L, I) 32

Toot-Toot! (T, L, I) 33

Making Friends at the Fair (E, F) 34

Hungry for Hot Dogs (H, E, F) 35

A Cozy Quilt (O, Q) 36

Cotton Candy (C, O, Q) 37

The Dunking Booth (B, D) 38

Feeding Time (G, B, D) 39

Rolling Roller Coaster (P, R) 40

Up, Up, and Away! (U, P, R) 41

Sack-Jumping (J, S) 42

Ant Antics (A, N) 43

Merrily We Go Around! (M, A, N) 44

What a Day! (V, W) 45

A Youthful Yawn (Y, V, W) 46

Can We Keep One? (K, X) 47

The Petting Zoo (Z, K, X) 48

Dear Parent:

Welcome to *Kindergarten: Tracing and Writing the ABC's!* This valuable tool is designed to help your child succeed in school. Scholastic, the most trusted name in learning, has been creating quality educational materials for school and home for nearly a century. And this resource is no exception.

Inside this book, you'll find colorful and engaging activity pages that will give your child the practice he or she needs to master essential skills, such as tracing lines and shapes, learning directionality, and tracing and writing upper- and lowercase letters A to Z.

To support your child's learning experience at home, try these helpful tips:

- Provide a comfortable, well-lit place to work, making sure your child has all the supplies he or she needs.

- Encourage your child to work at his or her own pace. Children learn at different rates and will naturally develop skills in their own time.

- Praise your child's efforts. If your child makes a mistake, offer words of encouragement and positive help.

- Display your child's work and celebrate his successes with family and friends.

We hope you and your child will enjoy working together to complete this workbook.

Happy learning!
The Editors

Petting-Zoo Pairs

Trace each line from a baby animal to its mother.

Pretty Ponies

Trace each line from a pony to its child.

A Rainy Day

Trace each line from top to bottom.

Big Balloons

Trace each line from
bottom to top.

Out Comes the Sun

Trace each line from top to bottom.

Colorful Kites

Trace each line from bottom to top.

Blowing Bubbles

Trace each circle. Start at the ●. Follow the ⟶ .

Clowning Around

Trace each circle. Start at the ●. Follow the ⟶ .

Wonderful Watermelons

Trace each curved line. Start at the ●. Follow the ⟶ .

Fun at the Fair

Trace each line. Start at the ● . Follow the ⟶ .

Lots of Licks

Trace and write.

Ticket Time

Trace and write.

If the weather is nice, go outside and draw straight lines on a sidewalk with large pieces of chalk.

Ooh! Aah!

Trace and write.

Dancing Dogs

Trace and write.

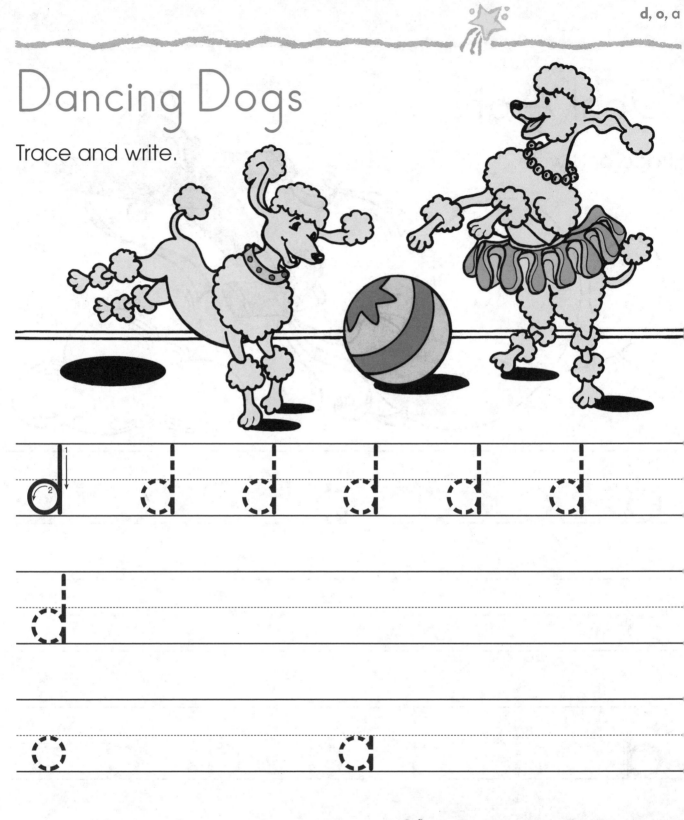

Crack! Splat!

Trace and write.

C C C C C C C C

C

e e e e e e e

e

Fancy Fireworks

Trace and write.

Spray some shaving cream on a cookie sheet. Spread out the shaving cream with your hands and use your pointer finger to draw letters in it.

Radiant Rainbow

Trace and write.

Time for a Nap

Trace and write.

n n n n n n n

n

u r

Go outside and practice writing letters in the sand or dirt with craft sticks.

n

Bouncing Balls

Trace and write.

3 Bounces
25¢

Perfect Pumpkins

Trace and write.

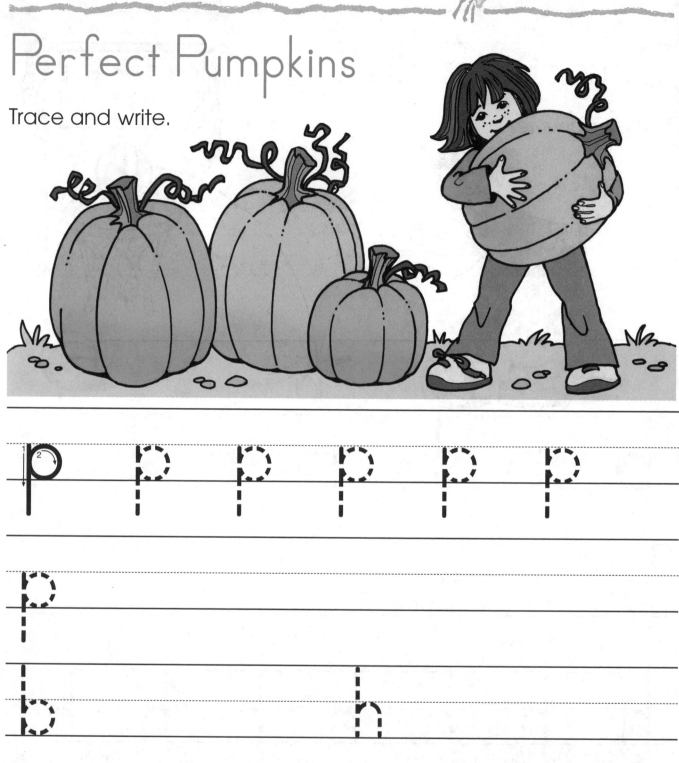

P P P P P

p

b   h

Fill plastic squeeze-type bottles with different colors of tempera paint. Squeeze the paint onto construction paper to create letters.

p

Jumping Goats

Trace and write.

g g g g g g

g

J J J J J J J

j

A Quarter a Quack

Trace and write.

QUACKING DUCKS • 25¢ EACH

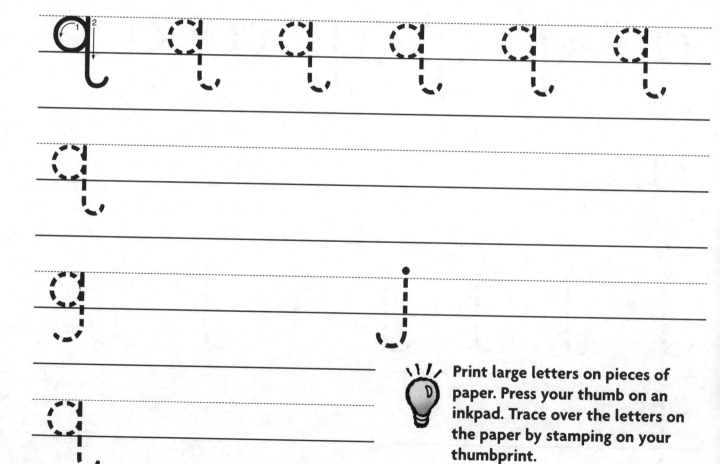

Print large letters on pieces of paper. Press your thumb on an inkpad. Trace over the letters on the paper by stamping on your thumbprint.

Music Makers

Trace and write.

A Vulture's Yo-Yo

Trace and write.

What Time Is It?

Trace and write.

W W W W W W

W

V Y

W

💡 **Practice forming letter shapes out of clay. Roll the dough into long strips and twist and turn the strips to form different letters.**

Box Kites

Trace and write.

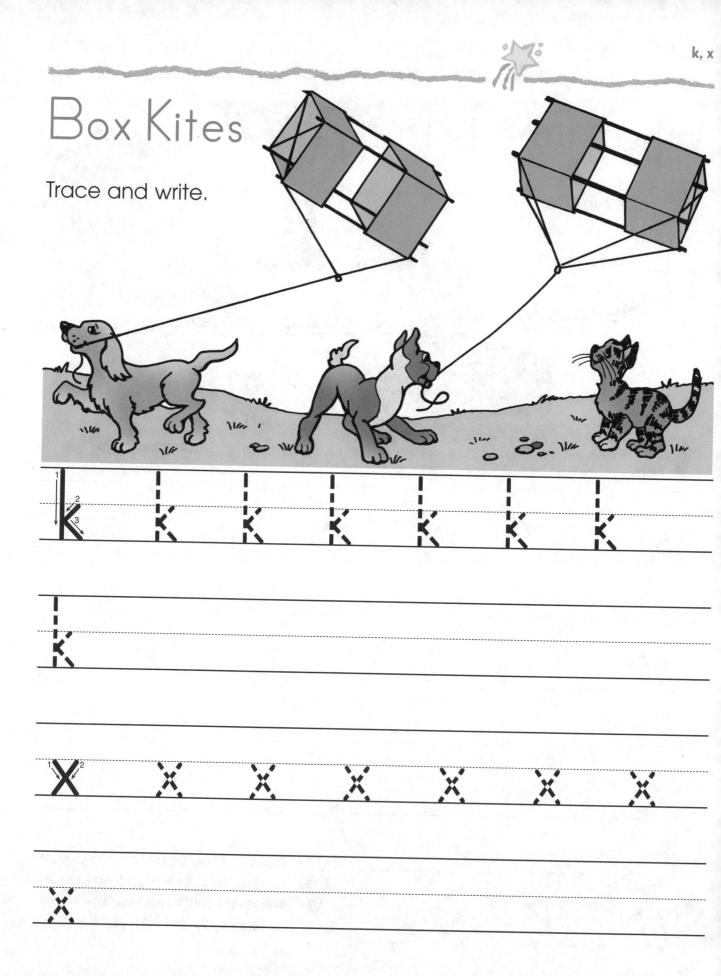

Zooming Along

Trace and write.

Z z z z z z z

z

k   x

 Practice forming letters using craft sticks. Glue your stick letters to construction paper.

z

Ice-Cold Lemonade

Trace and write.

Toot-Toot!

Trace and write.

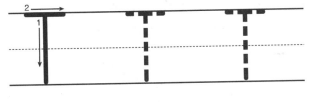

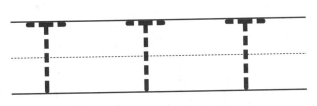

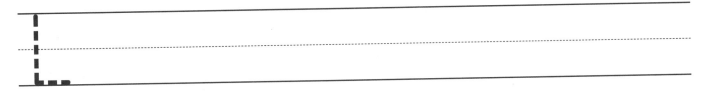

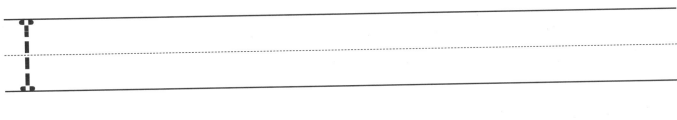

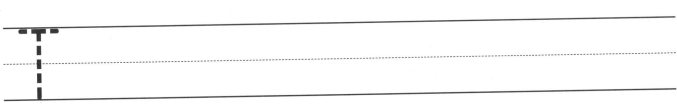

Making Friends at the Fair

Trace and write.

Hungry for Hot Dogs

Trace and write.

A Cozy Quilt

Trace and write.

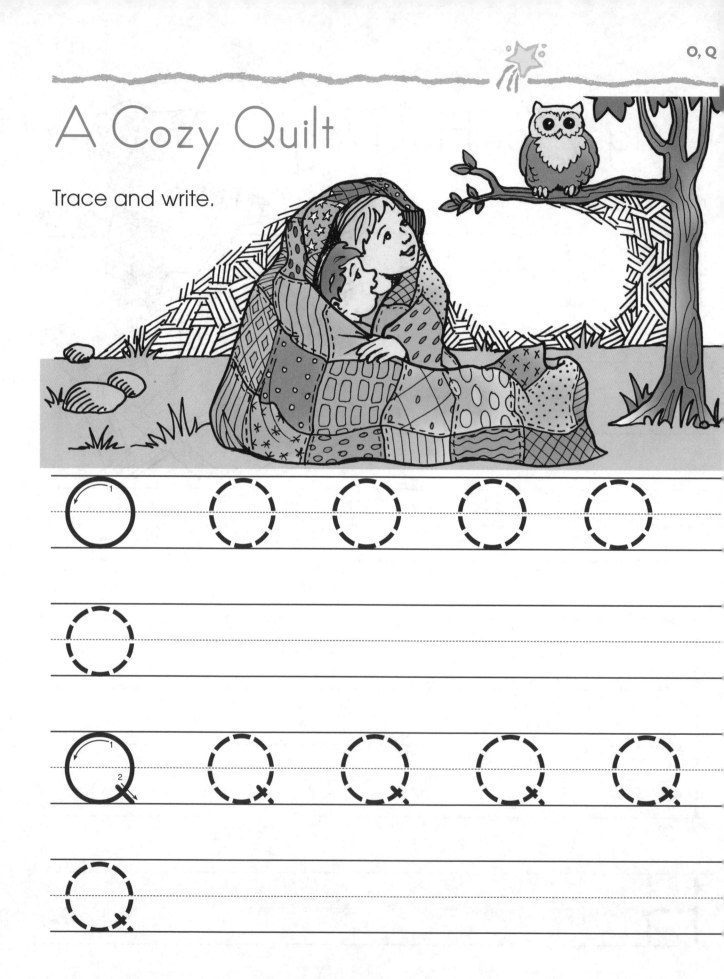

Cotton Candy

Trace and write.

C C C C

C C C

C

O

Q

C

The Dunking Booth

Trace and write.

Feeding Time

Trace and write.

G G G

G G G

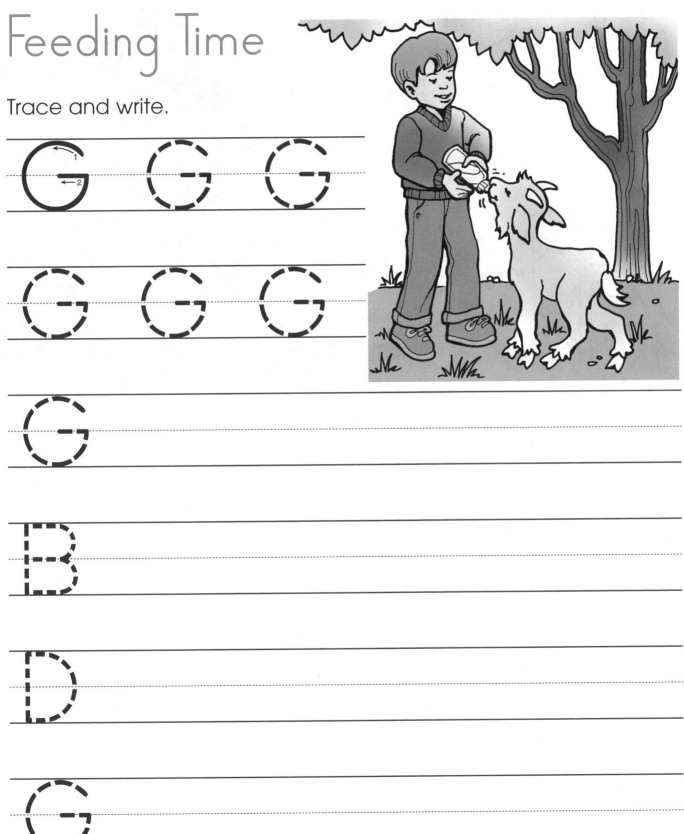

G

B

D

G

Rolling Roller Coaster

Trace and write.

P P P P P P P

P

R R R R R R R

R

Up, Up, and Away!

Trace and write.

U U U

U U U

U U U

P

R

U

Sack-Jumping

Trace and write.

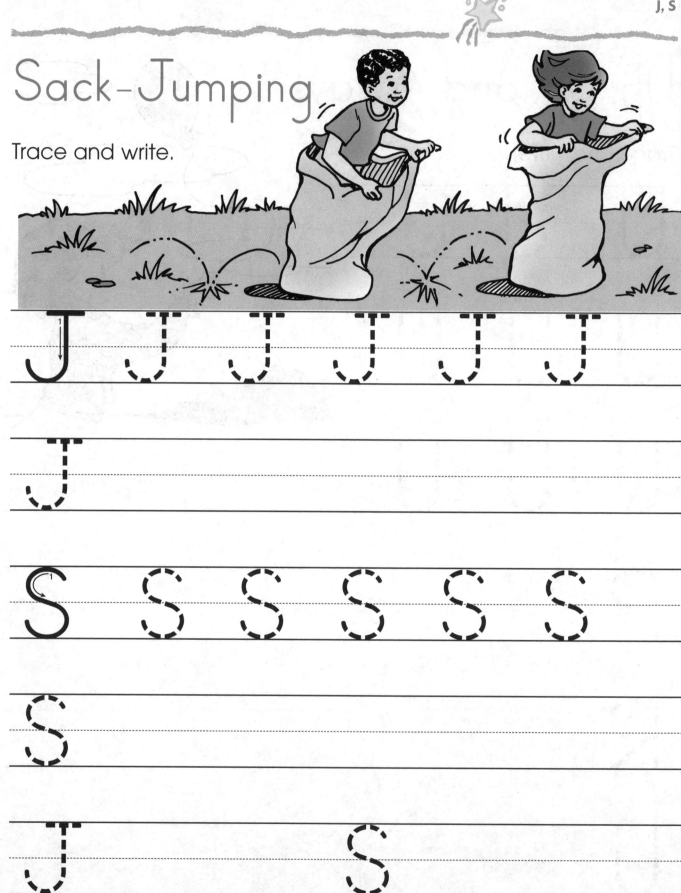

J J J J J J

J

S S S S S S

S

J   S

Ant Antics

Trace and write.

Merrily We Go Around!

Trace and write.

What a Day!

Trace and write.

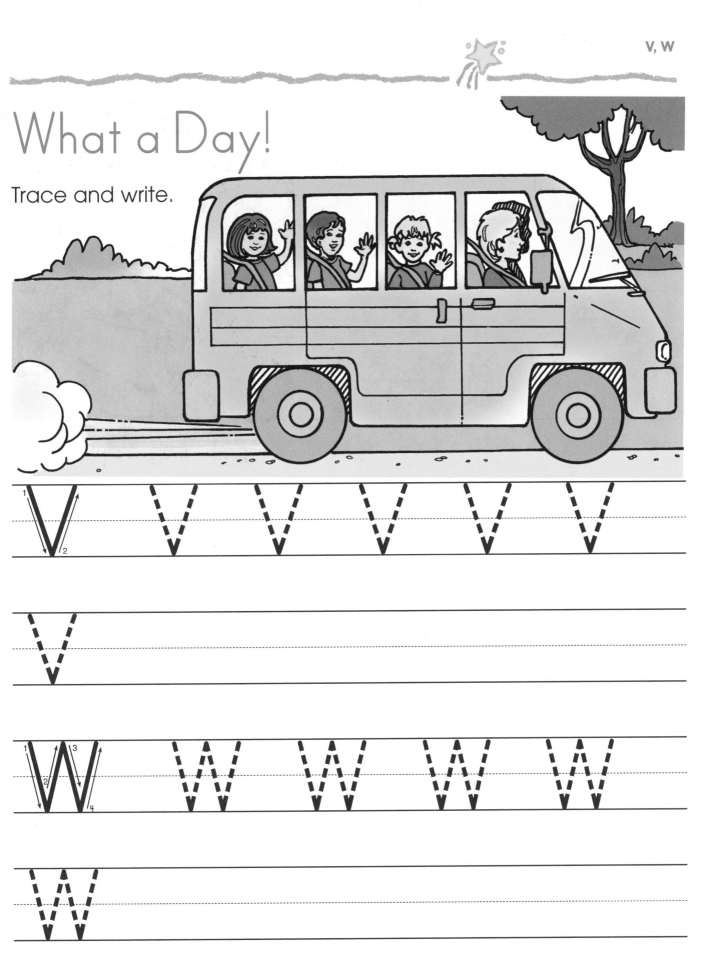

A Youthful Yawn

Trace and write.

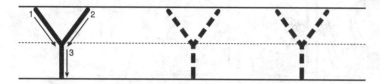

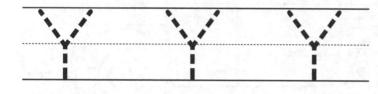

Can We Keep One?

Trace and write.

The Petting Zoo

Trace and write.

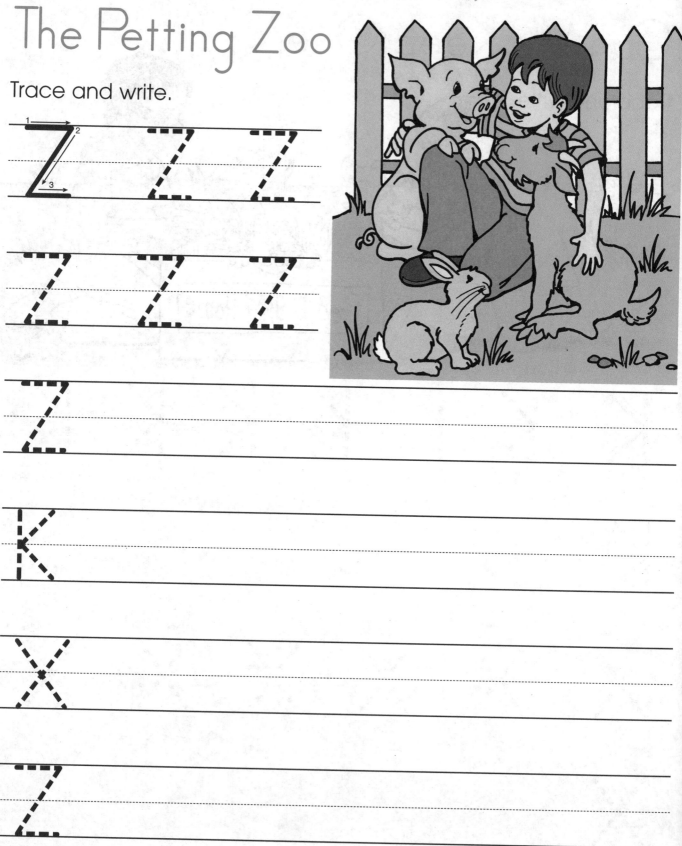